ROBERT L. O'BRIAN

MARSE JOE AND ME

New York City 2016

ISBN-13: 9781540613882
ISBN-10: 1540613887

For My Father

Prologue

My father, who turns 98 this May, is a far better man than I am in so many ways, far more considerate, outer-directed, multi-talented, helpful. He never desired to see his name up in lights or in an encyclopedia; he only cared about his family, friends, his work and his golf game—my dad's tastes and sensibilities are so streamlined, in fact, they don't extend to or include any form of music but Swing, any era of American history but that of his youth and early manhood, the era of the Great Depression and the Second World War, and but for his recent attachment to the Atlanta Braves, he remains nearly obsessed with the 1930s-40s New York Yankees. He was and to some extent yet remains a Man of "His Own" Time. While Dad's first instinct is to be helpful—he could build and fix *anything* and envisioned more than just stately mansions for his loved ones as the swift seasons tolled—he could not and would not submerge his identity enough to acquiesce to the fashions of later days and decades:

he might’ve admired the lyricism and exquisite melodic changes in the Beatles “Michelle,” or the piano on “L.A. Woman,”—“hey, that’s pretty good,” he’d comment while building or staining yet another bookcase (at one point, there appeared to be a fashion imperative to wear bell-bottoms without cuffs, too) but the electric heaviness of the harder rock musics would never win him over, no matter how hard we tried. On a summer day in 1972, as he was flipping hamburgers in our backyard, Dad said, “well, I’ve come to the conclusion that the Big Bands aren’t coming back.”

1972. After Woodstock. After the Democratic convention in Chicago and Manson. Gee, the Big Bands aren’t coming back.

What I’m saying is that while working on this book with my father, I had no doubt that he’d love and cherish reading and re-reading it. Memory, hither come. A glory has passed from the earth.

Robert Louis O’Brian was born in Buffalo, New York on May 8, 1919, the very day his Uncle Earl returned to the United States after a hellish tour of duty in World War I France. He met Joseph Vincent

"Marse Joe" McCarthy while delivering *The Buffalo Evening News* to the great Yankee manager and his wife, Elizabeth, who was known as "Babe." Pilgrims and sojourners travel to Rome, Mecca, Jerusalem, Yucatan, and to the Himalayas, and ingest psychotropic and mood-enhancing drugs to have my father's disposition. Engaged. Charismatic. Charming. Involved in mankind. Up to a point. The McCarthys took to the young kid from the icy cold town in Western New York and their friendship lasted for the rest of their lifetimes.

I'd be remiss not to mention two very good books about Marse Joe, whose fame, I believe, will only increase with each passing year: Richard J. Tofel's *A Legend in the Making: The New York Yankees in 1939* and Alan H. Levy's *Joe McCarthy: Architect of the Yankee Dynasty*, both at Amazon. Mr. Tofel asserts that Marse Joe McCarthy was major league baseball's greatest manager, an estimation with which my father and I agree.

One evening or two after this last Christmas, while I was visiting my father down in Western North Carolina, he insisted that Glenn Miller music was being played from one of the other apartments, perhaps on television. Next night, same thing.

"Somebody is playing Glenn Miller music," he insisted. He switched television stations. "Maybe *The Glenn Miller Story* is on TV."

"What song are they playing, Dad?" We were both sitting in big chairs.

"Moonlight Serenade," he answered. I still couldn't make out any of the song's strains. "You hear that?" he asked me.

"You know I can, Dad," I said. "I can hear it now, too. Yes. Yes. I can hear it, Dad. I can hear it . . ."

EYE OF THE MASTER

Was Joseph Vincent McCarthy the greatest major league baseball manager of all time? The wise men and women of today posit that, in this, the first decade of the 21st century, the age of extreme sports, reality TV and steroids, the national pastime has become all but irrelevant, thereby reducing our question, it would seem, to abject non-importance, but let's not forget: today's wisdom is often tomorrow's folly and baseball's obituary has been written before, most memorably in the 1960s when the Woodstock Nation and cosmic consciousness made the game seem quaint, if not downright reactionary. This was, after all, America's game and the Age of Aquarius would not brook allegiance to anything so patriotic, so bound by tradition, so uniform as baseball, much less to a team calling itself the Yankees.

Marse Joe McCarthy managed the New York Yankees from 1931 to 1946, steering them to eight American League pennants and to seven world championships. He also won a pennant for the Chicago Cubs in 1929, becoming the first manager to win pennants for teams in both leagues, a distinction that would hold for nearly sixty years. There are those who argue that McCarthy was baseball's greatest manager and for fifty years, he made Western New York his home. My father became friends with Marse Joe as a boy when he delivered *The Buffalo Evening News* to the McCarthy home at 52 Gates Circle in Buffalo during those grim early days of the Great Depression. McCarthy and his wife, Elizabeth, known as "Babe," never had children and at 13, my father became a kind of surrogate son to them. On cold afternoons when Dad was delivering the *Evening News*, Babe would often knock on her kitchen window and hold up a chicken leg or breast and motion for him to step inside for a hot meal while others, one can imagine, waited on bread lines across the country.

Nearly all of the characterizations and clichés of and about McCarthy were true. He was, in fact, reserved, meticulous, stern, all-business, fiercely competitive; obsessed, even. Olympian. A Pericles in knee-breaches and spikes, a strategic, even political genius in a world of jocks and sports page scribblers.

"Never a day went by when you didn't learn something from Joe McCarthy," said Joe DiMaggio.

But gushing he wasn't. When Babe died in 1971, I asked my father how Joe was holding up before my brother and I accompanied Dad to the funeral.

"He doesn't really say," Dad replied. "He's a great one for that, of course. Joe doesn't show his emotions."

Black Irish men rarely do—demonstrate emotion, that is—and it makes sense that the staid McCarthy chose a life attuned to Western New York's slower rhythm over the frenetic, insane pace of Manhattan. McCarthy attended Niagara University in 1906 and played minor league ball for the Buffalo Bisons way back in 1914 and fell in love with the area. ("It was just wilderness then," he once told *The Courier-Express*). Not until 1931, though, just after taking the reins as Yankee skipper, did he and Babe move to Gates Circle where they lived for a dozen years before buying the farm house on South Ellicott Creek Road in

Tonawanda—for $18,000!—in 1943. The white clapboard farm house on Ellicott Creek, now an historic landmark, was indeed, *finally*, home to the McCarthys, the last one that the couple, burnt-out after a quarter century of hotels and midnight trains, would inhabit. It was my great pleasure, as a youngster, to visit their house, which was filled up with bats, balls, uniforms, World Series rings, press pins and other memorabilia.

McCarthy was tough on his players and staff, known in the parlance of the day to "crack the whip" on occasion. In fact, the moniker "Marse" was, in white America's imagination, black English for "master." One supposes, then, that the Chicago sportswriter who gave McCarthy his most enduring nickname (early on, McCarthy was called "Busher Joe" as he was a bush leaguer, having never played in the major leagues himself) thought of Joe as a kind of slave driver, but there was a warm and ebullient, if not quite jovial, side to McCarthy as well. The old man waxed nostalgic about the days of vaudeville and, my father told me, never missed a segment of *The Pig and Whistle*, the Irish pub music and dance show featured on Canadian television in the 60s and 70s. Joe was close enough to George M. Cohan to serve as a pall-bearer at the Broadway song-and-dance genius's funeral at St. Patrick's Cathedral. Marse Joe could be delicate. This was not an insensitive man.

"He would never embarrass you in front of the other players," Phil "Scooter" Rizzuto remembered. "To me, McCarthy was the greatest manager ever."

McCarthy was also abidingly loyal to his ex-boss, William Wrigley, owner of the Chicago Cubs and Wrigley Field. Once, he handed out sticks of Wrigley's gum to my brother and me, saying "don't chew any other brand, boys," which struck us as odd because Wrigley fired McCarthy in 1930 after Joe's Cubs failed to win the World Series against the Philadelphia Athletics, managed by Connie Mack, the boyhood idol of the Philadelphia-born-and-bred McCarthy.

"Connie Mack was the greatest manager of all time," I heard Joe say more than once. "He managed the A's for *fifty* years. One team. Fifty years!"

"You're selling yourself short," my father always replied. "Don't kid yourself."

An enduring reverence for the magnificent, stiff-collared, Connie Mack is understandable but one can only speculate that McCarthy remained loyal to William Wrigley because it was the chewing gum tycoon who, in 1926, gave Marse Joe his first major league break after twenty years of playing, then playing and managing, for minor league teams in Buffalo, Wilkes-Barre, Dover (Delaware) and Louisville. (There could have been another, more mercenary reason: McCarthy owned Wrigley stock until the day he died.) In Chicago, McCarthy managed, among others, .400 hitter Rogers Hornsby, RBI great Hack Wilson and Grover Cleveland Alexander, an aging, temperamental prima donna who happened to be the third greatest pitcher of all time. Alexander, once empathetically portrayed on the screen by Ronald Reagan (Doris Day played his wife), was insolent and difficult and McCarthy didn't hesitate to fire the legend in his, McCarthy's, first year at the Chicago helm. Marse Joe took the last-placed Cubs to the National League championship in four years but lost to Philadelphia in just four games. Nevertheless, Chicago's loss was McCarthy's (and New York's) gain for just after Wrigley gave Joe the boot, a door opened in the Bronx, in New York, where McCarthy would achieve greatness yet grapple with another prima donna, the mythic, superhuman Babe Ruth.

They never got along. The Babe felt that *he* should have taken over as manager after the death of Miller Huggins and was a hulking mass of resentment for his last three seasons as a Yankee. But with Ruth's Promethean help, the Yankees won the World Series in 1932, after McCarthy's second season as manager, against, of all teams, the Chicago Cubs. This was the series in which Ruth, standing at home plate, famously pointed to the stands to indicate that the next pitch to him would be knocked into the Wrigley Field bleachers and it was. Or was it? McCarthy never baldly denied the veracity of this great urban legend, preferring instead to leave the matter of Ruth's prophetic powers to the fan's imagination.

"You believe what you want to believe," I heard Joe say—more than once—about that fabled day in October, 1932.

It was not all briars and thorns between McCarthy and the Bambino, however. One afternoon in the locker room, Ruth showed McCarthy a scorecard from 1914 which memorialized the day that the Babe, as a rookie pitcher for the Baltimore Orioles (then a minor league team; this was actually the *second* game in Ruth's professional career) struck out McCarthy four times—in Buffalo.

"Yes, but I was batting fourth," McCarthy answered Ruth who, as his jersey number indicated, always batted third in the lineup. "You never batted cleanup in your life!"

The player that McCarthy really loved, of course, was cleanup hitter Lou Gehrig who was in Joe's estimation, "a great ball player and an even greater person." While collecting for the *Evening News* on a Saturday afternoon, my father happened upon Gehrig at the Gates Circle apartment, carrying a tray of *hors d'oeuvres*.

“Have one of these goddamned things,” Lou said to my Dad. The idea of the Iron Horse saddled with a plate of tiny sandwiches and elegant finger food, surrounded by Dr. Dafoe (of Dionne Quintuplet fame) and writer Quentin Reynolds (who’d authored a favorite boyhood biography of Winston Churchill) was enough to capture my young imagination but that the wholesome, exemplary Gehrig, the Pride of the Yankees, would use the Lord’s name in vain—and in the presence of a teenager—always was and still is kind of shocking to me. You just never know about people. But another image of Gehrig is even more resonant and enduring. A portrait of Lou, the famous snapshot of the legendary first-baseman smiling by the batting cage, hung on one of McCarthy’s walls.

“I could tell Lou was starting to slip here,” said Joe in about 1971 as he pointed at the framed black-and-white portrait of his team captain. “I could see it in his neck.”

In his *neck*. McCarthy’s insight was deep. Penetrating. He studied his players’ psyches as well as their physical development so much so, that sportswriters began to titter about McCarthy’s psychological acumen. Joe, who knew nothing of Freudian slips but plenty about slides into second base, pooh-poohed all the talk of 'psychology,' although he certainly understood the importance and utility of positive thinking and an enhanced self-image.

"We carried ourselves like champions all the time," he said. "On and off the field." That's thinking outside the box, painting beyond the canvass. The road goes on forever. McCarthy's much-touted "Ten Commandments for Success in Baseball" also betrays a masterful insight into the physical and psychological make-up of his players; a mastery worthy of, say, a Zen master or, excuse me, a Zen "marse."

"Keep your head up," was his fourth commandment, "and you may not have to keep it down."

It was somewhat discomforting to have Marse Joe set his black eyes on you, even when they twinkled with mischief, this time as he asked my brother and me: "what is the most important rule in baseball?"

"Listen to the manager," my father said as my brother and I sat in stony silence, intimidated by the master himself.

"Keep your eye on the ball," Joe finally said. "At all times."

Well, it must be true, then: the eye is the lamp of the body. If thine eye be single, thy whole body will be full of light. Or full of World Series rings and champagne.

Writers and pundits do go on about the great American game, their prose purple with metaphors and assertions about baseball's place in American culture. Jacques Barzun of Columbia University famously said that whoever would know America had better know baseball. The rhetoric does get overblown but there is something about McCarthy and his achievement that is, if not of great historic significance, then at the least, singularly heroic and

American. Think about it: there are about two degrees of separation between Marse Joe McCarthy and Marilyn Monroe. Or would Joe DiMaggio count as just one degree? Seriously, though, you wouldn't be too far off to compare McCarthy, in one context, to Franklin D. Roosevelt whose star, like McCarthy's, shone brightest during the Depression and World War II. While FDR stumbled over his plan to pack the Supreme Court before regaining his powers in the late Thirties, McCarthy had three less than stellar years with the Yankees before winning four consecutive World Series championships between 1936 and 1940. McCarthy's Yankees garnered another World Series win in 1941, the year DiMaggio hit safely in 56 consecutive games, finishing off the Brooklyn Dodgers in five games just two months before Pearl Harbor. Yankee imperialism indeed.

You might liken Marse Joe to Harry Truman as well. Babe Ruth was McCarthy's Douglas MacArthur and neither Truman nor Marse Joe shrank from the challenge of facing a mortal icon who, while resplendent in his uniform and cap, couldn't quite see the forest for his own tree. The future of the team, the fate of the nation, were more important than the egos of two pampered prima donnas. Give 'em hell, Harry and Joe! There's something greater than Solomon here. Yet neither FDR, Truman nor even King Solomon in all his glory could have come up with the system of signals—the 'swing,' 'bunt,' 'steal,' 'take the pitch' body signs—devised by McCarthy. From the dugout, Marse Joe relayed signals to his third base coach who then used another set of signals to inform the batter or a runner as to how he should proceed and McCarthy's code was never cracked. Never. Like the Navajo lexicon used during World War II, McCarthy's system of signals remains arcane to this day, even to his friends and adopted family members.

"I could be sending a signal right now," the old man said during one of our Saturday afternoon visits. "Just sitting here in this rocker, I might be giving out a sign."

McCarthy retired from baseball in June 1950, in the middle of his third season with the Boston Red Sox.

"After losing the pennant in 1949 when we were so close," he told my Dad (the Bosox lost to the Yankees!), "I couldn't go on."

Failing health and disappointment finally sidelined the great tactician just as, ironically enough, another Joe McCarthy loomed over the American horizon. Isn't it funny that Marse Joe left baseball exactly four months after the junior senator from Wisconsin first announced that he held "in his hand" a list of Communists and suspected traitors, variable in number? Our Joe McCarthy emanated hope and light but the other one cast a dark shadow over the republic as we all know. Still, Marse Joe was not immune to the prejudices and bigotry of his day.

"In Cooperstown, there's an old high school named James Fenimore Cooper High School," he once told us. "It has this real proper impressive lettering. 'James Fenimore Cooper High School' it reads in gold letters." McCarthy smiled wide at us. "Nothing but blacks!" he exclaimed with a caustic, high-pitched laugh. "All blacks!" In this vein, Joe, sounding much like Don Imus, told my father that veteran Negro League and later major league pitcher Satchel Paige required only "a bottle of whisky and two women" to stay happy.

"Yep," he cackled, "a bottle of whisky and two women."

McCarthy did not have kind words, either, for Jim Bouton, the Yankee pitcher and author of the frank and irreverent *Ball Four* which, while hilarious and witty to the Now Generation, angered die-hard Yankee fans.

"Joe says Bouton is no good," my father announced from our dinner table in Amherst.

McCarthy cared little for Bouton's literary prowess and, one feels certain, would not have bothered to read the sequel to *Ball Four* as Marse Joe never tolerated a player or a writer who made the same mistake twice. ("I don't speak to McCarthy," one journalist said, "unless I have to.") But Marse Joe probably cared even less for Bouton's groovy hairstyle as he once said to my brother and me one day as we departed, "get a haircut!" Now, this is a funny memory, firstly because Joe laughed when he enjoined us to trim our Seventies locks but secondly, and even more to the point, my brother's and my hair barely touched our ears at that time.

Here are some desultory facts and recollections about McCarthy that may interest readers from Western New York and beyond. He thought little of the designated hitter rule, introduced in 1972. "It'll only benefit the pitchers" he opined from his living room. And speaking of hirsuteness, Joe's own hair never turned gray or white. It remained naturally coal-black, as black as his Irish eyes, until the day he died in January 1978 at the age of 90. He smoked big cigars, I can't recall the brand, and always wore a blue or red flannel shirt when we visited. He gave my father one of Babe Ruth's Yankee caps which remained in Dad's bottom drawer for decades until it was sold during the sports memorabilia craze of the early Nineties. A team photograph taken in Louisville in 1921 revealed that the young Joe McCarthy had a very handsome, almost classic face. Square jaw, you know. Like seeing photos of Grover Cleveland or William McKinley in their youth, you're surprised that these men once had looks that were quite prepossessing. It must be a Buffalo thing.

More recollections: one day, my father went alone to see Joe who told him, "You just missed Ted Williams. He left ten minutes ago." Joe managed Williams, perhaps the greatest natural hitter of all time, while with Boston. My father did meet DiMaggio, though. Only once, when the Yankee Clipper was just a rookie. It was in the Hollenden Hotel in Cleveland and my father says he was more interested in his strawberry shortcake than in meeting the unknown from San Francisco. I first met McCarthy at my grandfather's funeral in 1966, at a funeral home on Hertel Avenue. I sat on his lap. I was seven years old. Finally, my brothers and I never met McCarthy's wife. Not even once. Babe was confined to her bed upstairs and one time Joe said, "all right, boys, you stay here while I take your father up to see Mrs. McCarthy." As the bedroom door creaked open upstairs, we could hear Babe's demented babbling, an endless stream of la-la-la's, yet she did smile, Dad told me, when reminded of the chicken pieces she held aloft in her kitchen window so many years before. But Dad's final visit with Babe McCarthy about a year later was different.

"She didn't even know who I was," he said evenly.

If humanity really is a kind of golden ball of spirit rather than a collection of individuals, then the Woodstock Nation was more or less on point: all you need is love. The irascible Ted Williams was candid about his feelings for the Sage of Ellicott Creek.

"I loved Joe McCarthy," wrote Williams in his autobiography, echoing the sentiments of Gehrig, DiMaggio, Bill Dickey, Scooter Rizzuto and a thousand others. But this was not the slobbering, sentimental, ultimately superficial love of hippies and suitcase preachers on the make. This was, rather, the love and devotion of the general-statesman; a magnanimity fused with a kind of Celtic stoicism that once made men out of boys and winners, champions, out of those temporarily at a loss. The word 'inspire' means 'to breathe into' and Marse Joe McCarthy was nothing if not inspired and inspiring, breathing life into faltering, stagnant teams. He was not a father in the biological sense, but Gehrig, DiMaggio, Ted Williams as well as my own father were just four of his sons. And if, again, humanity is, in truth, a kind of shining golden ball rather than a roster of individual players, then we really are all on the same team. McCarthy knew that it is by striving unselfishly for the greater good, by being a team player, that one realizes one's individual greatness but was Marse Joe really the greatest manager of all time?

McCarthy is yet the winningest manager in baseball history with a .614 winning percentage, still a record. He never finished out of the first division. Not ever. Critics, however, carped that anyone could win with the talent that Colonel Jacob Ruppert, the brewer, the George Steinbrenner of his day, acquired for the Yankee organization.

"Yes, they called me a push-button manager," Joe once said to us dourly as he chomped on a cigar. Then he winked. "But I knew what buttons to push."

Look at Casey Stengel. While it is true that Stengel won ten pennants as Yankee manager, one more than Joe's nine, you'll notice that Stengel never won with any other team. As manager of the hapless Boston Braves and the even less amazing New York Mets of the early Sixties, the Old Perfessor was powerless, so the critics were wrong; those counted wise in their time usually are. Whether at Chicago, New York or Boston, Joe McCarthy did not merely or randomly push buttons. He never finished out of the first division. As true wisdom is a first cousin of vision (think of 'vizier,' and *wissenschaft*), I wonder how today's game, with its cocaine and steroids scandals, would appear to Marse Joe's ever-watchful eye. I would want to ask him: Will baseball sink into irrelevance? Will it throw in the towel? What signs can you give us, Joe? Can't you just give us a *sign*??? I think, as an answer, McCarthy might just repeat one of his own commandments. For those who've managed to make contact.

"Always run them out," he would say. "You can never tell."

More sage advice, more wisdom from Western New York's own Marse Joe McCarthy, the man who never took his eye off the ball.

Reprinted from Western New York Heritage Magazine, *June 2007*

MARSE JOE & ME

NY
NEW YORK
1932

Dad, how exactly did you meet Marse Joe?

It would've been about 1931 or 2, Son, the year he began building the house on Gates Circle. I was their paperboy and they were very nice to me. They had no children, I don't know why, I never found out, but they sort of adopted me, in fact, I saw more of Babe, his wife, than I saw of Joe. She was very lonely when he was on the road. She'd travel with him occasionally, but only so much. My mother and Babe took a road trip once to New York City to shop. They stayed in the New Yorker, I think. The New Yorker Hotel near Penn Station.

Where Tesla died?

Ha! That's funny. Yes. Where Tesla died. You're going back to my Westinghouse days. Mother and Babe drove to New York from Buffalo, just the two of them, in that old black Packard Joe bought. One Sunday when I was about thirteen, it was winter, I grabbed on to the rear tire, the exposed rear tire with the cover, you know, as Joe and Babe were driving away from St. Joseph's Cathedral on

Sunday for mass. Main and Utica, city of Buffalo. I held on to the tire and made it, skating on the ice, all the way to their place on Gates Circle, which had no garage, by the way. There was no room for one. Joe was very angry with me. "Bobby, don't ever do that again!" he said. They were in their Sunday best. I idolized him. He was my hero. But he yelled at me. Boy, he was mad. And it was cold! I remember *that*. Every Christmas, I'd bring calendars to my news customers expecting a big tip and Joe never tipped me. I don't know why. Maybe, he didn't know about the custom.

You once said that by Christmas, Marse Joe was already in Florida for spring training.

Not *that* early. Usually, I'd get a dollar, sometimes, even five dollars for Christmas tips, for the Christmas calendar, from the other customers, all newsboys would, and this was during the Depression. My mother rented one of our bedrooms for a dollar night. Her boarders were relatives and friends of patients staying at Millard Fillmore Hospital across the street. That's where I was born.

My brother and I had to give up our bedroom and sleep in the attic. We didn't care. But my father didn't even have a car. Can you imagine? He took buses to sell insurance. The bus! As he was coming home one evening, my mother said to me, "you know your father had only an apple for lunch today." I never forgot that. Obviously. I still tear up thinking about it.

What were some of the things you and others, kids and adults, did for money at that time?

When I was about ten, in 1929 or so, before the Crash, I worked for a man who drove a horse-drawn carriage to deliver cakes and bread. I can still see him now, driving along Delaware Avenue in that horse-and-buggy. I clipped some tulips, some flowers, from a woman's garden, then rang her doorbell and sold them to her. She bought them! I think she knew my ruse, but she went along anyway. My brother and I delivered newspapers, *The Buffalo Evening News*, and there was a contest in '32: whoever could get twelve new subscriptions would win a trip to Cleveland to see the Indians play the Yankees in their new stadium, Briggs Stadium. I ran down, literally ran, to the foot of Main Street to turn in my new subscriptions. I ran there to be the first one and I was. Some other boys took the train with me to Cleveland. We stayed at the Hollenden Hotel. The game was rained out, so we were told we could stay an extra day in Cleveland for the double-header on Saturday or Sunday and the Yanks lost both games! Joe hated that, hated to lose. Anyway, we had great seats on the first-base line and Joe waved at the *News* guy, the *Buffalo Evening News* rep, then at me, and motioned for me to come down to the dugout where I met Ruth, Gehrig, Dickey, Lefty Gomez, and in the hotel later, young rookie, DiMaggio. The photo of me shaking hands with Joe in the dugout was taken in Cleveland and that snapshot appeared on the front page of the second section of the Sunday *News*. I was very proud of myself. And of Joe. I was protective of him and Babe, too. One time, this kid, I'll never forget it, Billy Hubble was his name . . . this kid insulted Babe, called her fat, I think, and I reprimanded him; and he apologized after I told him who she was. I got off my bike and told him to apologize, right there on Gates Circle, and he did! He walked up to her and apologized. He was wearing a big fur coat and was twice my size, too. I can still see it. We'd often see Joe and Babe walking from church on Sundays, walking from St. Joseph's Cathedral. They were serious Catholics. Very devout. At first, they rented a flat upstairs on the circle, then they built that apartment before moving out to the country during the war. Then, I'd drive out to visit. I never saw Joe manage when he was with Boston. I tried to get to the playoffs—Joe tried to get tickets for your mother and me in 1949, those playoff games against the Yankees, but couldn't. He was treated terribly in Boston. By everyone. The front office, the players, the press. He'd had enough after three years or so. But, I'll never forget that he made $52,000 a year during the Depression. A thousand dollars a week. During the Depression!

You had a Jewish girlfriend during the Depression. That was a big deal then . . .

Yes. Irene Rosenberg. Her parents were nice, I liked them, but we still had to kind of lie, so, my friend, Irv Rubin, who was going out with a girl named Jean Ranahan, would switch with me on Saturday nights when we'd go out. Irv would pretend he was taking out Irene, and I would pretend I was taking out Jean. I worked with Irv, too, at the Goody Cake Shop at Elmwood and Hodge. The Rosenbergs ate ham, by the way, and when their parents dropped by unexpectedly, Irene's grandparents, Mrs. Rosenberg came over to our house and gave us the ham she was baking. Funny. My German grandfather from Pittsburgh, Jake Mohn, came to live with us in the early-mid-Thirties and he'd ask me, "are you still going out with that Jew girl?" He was a nice guy, though. You would've liked him.

Before the war and up until the time you enlisted in the Army Air Corps in 1943, you worked as a mechanic, then as a field representative for Curtiss-Wright, the aircraft company, traveling to Iran, India, South Africa, then, domestically, to Salt Lake City, Los Angeles, New York. Were you still in contact with Marse Joe at this time?

When Curtiss went on strike, I worked out of their office in downtown Buffalo, in the Ellicott Square Building. I was outside, smoking a cigarette with Howard Ray, who went to Iran with me, when Joe walked by. We said hello. After the war, I took your mother over to the place on South Ellicott Creek Road to meet Joe and Babe. We'd invite them over for dinner, but they refused. You remember, of course, when I invited Joe over for Christmas dinner after Babe died. Remember? Spaghetti and meatballs? That was his favorite. But he didn't come.

I remember it well. Christmas 1971.

One time, not long before that Christmas, I stopped by Joe's place without first telephoning. He said "you just missed Ted Williams. He just left." Ted Williams! I'd take you boys over to see him, of course, get some autographs, take some pictures. He gave me a number of his World Series rings and press passes, press pins, too. Remember that huge pantry in the South Ellicott house? I wonder what the place looks now. That Cadillac . . . the '59 Fleetwood in his garage with the huge whitewall tires. He offered it to me, you know . . . he wanted to give it to me, his mint-green 1959 Fleetwood Cadillac, but it was too big. I didn't want it. I'd call him once in a while, too, and he came to Dad's funeral, but we were in sporadic contact. We knew some wealthy people, even during the Depression, but Joe was different. Always on the road. One family over on St. James Place had a turntable in their garage—do you know what that is? They'd drive into the garage, their big coupe or sedan, then the turntable would turn the car around to face the garage door and driveway. No backing out of the driveway. The Clements lived in one of the Delaware Avenue mansions. I knew Norman Clement from Boy Scouts. We called him "Nummy." They were nice people, very wealthy, had a beautiful summer home in East Aurora, beautiful; two maids, a chauffeured Packard, finger bowls at the dinner table. They had money. Mr. Clement liked me, too, because after the war, he said he could pull some strings and get me into Yale with a scholarship. I was all set to go, but, then, I thought I'd be too old when I graduated, 29, and I turned him down. He was disappointed. Can you believe it? I was a high school drop-out. I worked odd jobs, went back to school, graduated at 20, then got the job at Curtiss-Wright, went overseas, only to turn down a scholarship to Yale. What was I thinking? But, I wouldn't have met your mother, I don't think. You wouldn't be sitting here right now.

You told me that Joe liked The Pig & Whistle *on Canadian TV. And* Hee-Haw.

He loved the old songs, traditional music, and the papers said that Joe "mourned the passing of vaudeville." Buffalo was a great vaudeville town, but that was before my time, really. Joe was like my parents when it came to the more modern stuff. The Big Bands, for example: they said, "it all sounds the same." (*laughs*)

Tell us, if you would, about your time with Curtiss-Wright, going overseas, and then your stint in the Army Air Corps.

I started out as a mechanic for Curtiss in '39, when the plant was on Elmwood Avenue in Kenmore. My first car was a 2-door black Ford coupe with a rumble seat, in fact, I was driving that one or the red Plymouth, driving with my girlfriend, Helen, when we heard about the Pearl Harbor attack on the car radio. We'd never heard of Pearl Harbor and Hitler was pretty much unknown to me. I cared about baseball, cars and girls, not politics, really. I first went overseas in February 1942. We stopped in Capetown, South Africa and in India, Bombay, but I never made it to the Taj Mahal. I could shoot myself. We worked in small barracks in Abadan, Iran and it was very hot, not a great place, but a great experience. We were assembling P-40s and C-46's, "P" for pursuit planes and "C" for cargo planes. We were building them for the Soviets, maybe the British, too, the "allies," you know, and they'd come to Abadan and pick 'em up. We worked with Bell Aircraft, too, and Douglass. We would test fly them, not me, but our pilots would. I met the brother of a friend of mine, Amy Chenovsky, in Abadan. "You're from Buffalo? Your last name is Chenovsky? Do you know

Amy?" "She's my sister." It was like that. When my brother was in Hawaii during the war, he met our cousin, Abbott Mohn. I was overseas for a year, then was sent to Salt Lake City, where I had a lush job. I think I played golf most of the time, 54 holes in one day! When the boss from Buffalo came to the plant, I happened to be working hard; he sees me in a C-46 that needed a valve replaced or something. I was down in the belly of the aircraft and he thought I worked this hard all the time. I lucked out. I almost got engaged to a girl, a Mormon girl, named Lorraine Petersen. Her family called her "Pete" and her little sister, "Re-Pete." Isn't that funny? She was going to convert to Roman Catholicism, studying the sacraments and all that, but then it faded. I left. Went back to my girlfriend, Helen, in Buffalo. And I felt guilty, too. I felt guilty about the guys going overseas and dying, so I enlisted. Some friends of mine, schoolmates from Lafayette High School, were killed in the war. Joe Kalbfleisch, Bob Weir. Nice guys. I was all set to be a flight engineer on a B-29, then the war ended. I didn't meet my brother in Hawaii for New Year's Eve as we had planned, but that was okay. The war was over. Did you know that when I was working for Curtiss-Wright in LA, I met my brother at the Ambassador Hotel? We swapped clothes. I wore his captain's uniform so I could go to this officer's dance and he took mine. I could've been arrested for impersonating an officer and your Uncle Bill would've been in big trouble, too. You know who I danced with? At the Ambassador Hotel? Barbara Hale. Della Street from *Perry Mason*. I even drove her home. One day, I drove down to Pittsburgh, California and saw a sign in front of an office building, I forgot what it was, but I remember what the sign said: "Soldiers and Dogs keep off the lawn." Can you believe that? Curtiss-Wright never made the transition to jet aircraft, though. I'm not sure what they do now.

Your brother, Bill, came home from Okinawa where he saw action. You always said he was despondent, never spoke about it; sat alone looking out the bay window in the sun room of your house.

People matured after their war experiences. My brother was in 101st Searchlight Division, I think it was something like that. Searchlight Battalion, maybe. Sat in Mother's and Dad's sun room on Wellington Road and never talked about it. I guess people became more serious. It was a very serious time. What was it all for, though? What were we fighting for? Businessmen. Politicians. They're all phony. They all lie. War is hell, it shouldn't be glorified, but Bell Aircraft built the P-51s and I sat in the cockpit one day in Buffalo when I shouldn't have and could've been clobbered, in big trouble. Maybe it was in Iran. I was dying to fly that thing.

Did you and Joe discuss politics? Did he ever mention Senator *Joe McCarthy?*

No. We didn't. It never came up. He didn't like Jim Bouton, I know that—not that he was political, strictly. He read *The Sporting News*, loved living out in Getzville, in the country, and took care of Babe. He almost put her in a home, but didn't have to, finally. I thought Ted Williams would attend the funeral or DiMaggio, but they didn't, not even Joe's funeral. I didn't even attend Joe's funeral. I was responsible for moving our division of Westinghouse down to North Carolina. I couldn't go. It was small, though. No family. The players were old. Down in Florida. I felt bad for Babe. That she got so sick. She really loved seeing me come up the driveway when I was a kid, delivering papers. Politics? I don't think Joe cared that much.

What was the greatest thing you learned from Marse Joe McCarthy?

Babe Ruth's hat.

Wait . . .

I had that hat for years. I even painted the house while wearing it in the early Fifties and got white speckles on it. I shouldn't have done that. Another regret! (*laughs*) The hat with the tag on it. "B. Ruth." Joe gave me an entire uniform once, a Yankee uniform and I had it up in our attic when I went overseas and when I came back in the fall of 1945? It was gone. We moved from Oxford Avenue to Wellington Road during the war and I'm almost sure one of the movers got it. Yup. Stole it. I never saw it again. The day I came to collect, as a paperboy, the day I met Gehrig and Dr. Dafoe, Joe promised to get me a poster or something, maybe Babe said it—promised to get me all their autographs but I never did get it. Quentin Reynolds. Lefty Gomez. But they'd given me enough. This is funny: when I knocked on a hotel door in Cleveland back in '32, a room I thought was Joe's, Wiley Post answered. Remember him? The one-eyed aviator who crashed with Will Rogers? He answered the door, took one look at me and said, "what do *you* want?" Not so friendly. I finally found Joe's room and he was in his long underwear! "Bobby, you'll have to come back later," he said. He had some meetings, too. Later, my brother and I got to meet Babe Ruth. We went up and touched him. When Uncle Bill and I left for Cleveland, or maybe it was Chicago, my father asked, "boys, do you need any money?" "No, Dad," we answered, "we have fifty cents each." Fifty cents!

Dad, I meant . . . what lesson did you learn from him? From your years of friendship?

Always treat friends and associates with respect. That's the key. Respect.

Ten Commandments for Success in Baseball by Joe McCarthy (1949)	
#	Commandment
1.	Nobody ever became a ballplayer by walking after a ball.
2.	You will never become a .300 hitter unless you take the bat off your shoulder.
3.	An outfielder who throws in back of a runner is locking the barn after the horse is stolen.
4.	Keep your head up and you may not have to keep it down.
5.	When you start to slide, slide. He who changes his mind may have to change a good leg for a bad one.
6.	Do not alibi on bad hops. Anybody can field the good ones.
7.	Always run them out. You never can tell.
8.	Do not quit.
9.	Do not fight too much with the umpires. You cannot expect them to be as perfect as you are.
10.	A pitcher who hasn't control hasn't anything.

Made in United States
North Haven, CT
09 July 2026

14138420R00033